Peter,

Seed by seed, word by word, Poem by poem. On the path together. I cherish our friendship.

With love and affection

Kathryn

October 2021

SEED WHEEL

poems Kathryn Hunt

Kathryn

LOST HORSE PRESS
Sandpoint, Idaho

ACKNOWLEDGMENTS

All We Can Hold (anthology): "The Summer You Imagined Me," "My First Garden"
Bluestem: "Now That Mornings Are Cold Again"
Bracken: "That Willow"
Carolina Quarterly: "My Dead Speak—to Me. Do Yours—to You?," "Cycling," "Dr. Kildare"
Coal Hill Review: "Road Trip"
Crab Creek Review: "Do You Consider Yourself a Nature Poet?"
Frontier: "What Rituals Did You Perform?"
Fugue: "Drift, Boat"
The Madrona Project: Keep a Green Bough: Voices from the Heart of Cascadia (anthology): "Ash-Boat"
Missouri Review: "Yellowstone" (Poem of the Week), "What Is to Be Done?," "The Journalism Student 1968," "Family History," "Fire in the North Country," "Domestic Animals"
Narrative: "What Do the Hands Remember?" (Poem of the Week)
Naugatuck River Review: "Where Are Your Gloves, Anna?"
Orion: "Spring Equinox," "Winter Solstice"
Poetry Northwest: "An Offering"
Radar: "Avatar," "Talking Like This"
Rappahannock Review: "Reading Hamlet," "Water Children"
Raven Chronicles: "Letter Home"
RHINO: "Ursa Major Prowls the Chugach Range"
Shark Reef: "Telling Time"
Terrain: "The Old Country," "Migrations"
Willow Springs: "Last Changes," "Gravel Road"

Cover Photograph: Camille Seaman, *Tracks Through the Field*, Kansas, May 2008.
Author Photo: Ronda Piszk Broatch.
Book Design: Christine Lysnewycz Holbert.

FIRST EDITION

This and other fine LOST HORSE PRESS titles may be viewed on our website at www.losthorsepress.org.

LIBRARY OF CONGRESS CATALOGING-IN-PUBLICATION DATA
Cataloging-in-Publication Data may be obtained from the Library of Congress.
ISBN 978-1-7364323-0-3

for Geo, always

CONTENTS

I Road Trip

II The Country I Come From

III Migrations

Road Trip

TALKING LIKE THIS

for Andrea Carlisle

A cold wind blew in gusts that caught
the root-hold of the firs. Clouds fled across the sky
and I felt empty, free of myself, just walking.
The way the trees leaned and circled, tossing
their long branches like a woman who's
had enough might toss away something
she loves.

A few doors down men were putting up
a wall with their nail guns and saws.
Ladders, bags of sand all over the yard.
How satisfying that must feel, to stand back
at the end of the day and admire a house
you've made in the company of others.
To be of practical use, like a frying pan.

Don't fall off your ladders, I shouted.
Each one some mother's child. I'm not
a mother myself, but I had a wish
to remind them. I was afraid they'd fall off
in a blast of cold wind. And they waved at me,
maybe not hearing my words at all.

My friend was out in her yard—
she gathered her cat in her arms and
stood with me. The wind blew round us,
pushing us this way and that. She tucked her
cat inside her sweater.
I feel a deep anger about something I can't

quite exactly pin down, she said.
I know, I said.
A big wet cloud falling over me.
Yes, I said. I pulled my hat tighter
down over my ears.

I grow weary of my mind's limitations,
my indecision, she said. The feeling that
everything is slowing down.
How much it hurts.
Aging, death, the whole thing.

I get that, I said.
I can't fight against it any longer, she said.
No, I said, won't do you much good.
Still, she said, I treasure each
chance we have to talk like this.
That matters, doesn't it.

The wind took up her voice then,
raked it over the backbones of
the firs, swept it far off
into another country.

AN OFFERING

Animals come down through stars
to reach the valley. A coyote with
its nose pressed in a rabbit hole.
Two Sandhill cranes as tall as rain,
and listening north. And when a cougar
screams its human scream, I'm suddenly
a child again, awake, the parched air
raked by drumfire blasts, window panes
all gleam and vast, animals angling
through ripe alfalfa fields. My grandmother
holding me to the thunder-headed sky
as if I were an offering. Saying, There,
see how meager we are made. How
our bones ring with fury and light.

MY DEAD SPEAK—TO ME. DO YOURS—TO YOU?

Death draws a line beneath,
straight and neat; a life in sums
of days—given, chanced, withstood,
embraced. What came and was
and where the old road turned
and when a hat was left behind
after a visit.

Last night a Snowy owl flew up,
startled from a hedge of Nootka
rose. Its eyes shone with
a moan of light. I watched that
solemn hunter gain against gravity,
lift, veer, and disappear. Its wings
seethed, and slashed the air. I
looked up—wild to see it go.

WHAT IS TO BE DONE?

for S. Reddick, 1976

I'll answer your question now, the one you asked that
evening we sat in your room, the hotplate you never used,
not even for coffee. Windows filmed with the dust of voices
that reached us years later. The river was weeds. The sentinel
towers of the canneries and sawmills that crowded
its banks. The graveyard hours you stood on the peach line,
the corrugated light. Women and men in white aprons
roaming through warehouses, trailing the sun.

None of us knew the way out of suffering. Who could escape
the torrent of heat that surged over our bodies and houses
like a dream? Our lovers' kids slept open-mouthed
on damp sheets while we wrote in small notebooks,
discovering the ruins of sky, the moment of falling
always in us. The world was on fire, each of us
on fire. Empires trolled over the earth, their
monstrous wheels. We argued power, revolution,
melodic rebellion. Bewailed the girls we'd loved without
claim, the ones who left town in bad-mannered cars.
Our own country becoming Rome in the beautiful
devouring flare of youth once given.

The mind returns to its sorrows by habit, like a waitress
counting out pennies at the end of her shift. There
it builds its glorious city of losses. Old friend,
moonlight climbs over the hills tonight, while I write
you this letter. The fires will keep burning,
I see that now. And how small the gestures of thought,
how immense the silence between words. We recited

Whitman and Ginsberg while our clothes tumbled
in a laundromat dryer. I remember the consoling
ring of our coins as they dropped in the slots, the music,
the real blessing of that. Soon enough our lives would show us
how all is torn away, dying moment by moment
to become something else. Leaving only heat,
and the wind-burnt leaves.

THE JOURNALISM STUDENT 1968

We lived by column inches, hermetic
deadlines, the pleasure of our names
above the fold. Hunched over stand-up
tabletops, our fingers capped with cooling wax,
we wielded dull Xacto knives, pressed yards
of adjective-free copy to the page
with rubber rollers. Conjured images
in a closet in the basement, a red light
to let secret lives float up, unharmed,
in dark. Our photographs, small
flags in black and white.

One afternoon the Jurassic,
woolly-scented teacher said to me,
You'll have a scholarship,
the letter's here. She waved it in
the gluey air. That meant I'd go to
college and whatever that would be.

On that day, I was a girl, a receiver,
who would tell you now I've never
understood enough, can only faintly
see the sacred hearts of others
and all that matters in this marveled,
savage world. The ruined empires
of the poor. A burning girl
running through a photograph forever.
The faces of men, of women, broken
open by their wanting.

On that lonesome afternoon I turned
back to our tables, our last brave words
finally staked to paper, our pages off to press.
An unread letter on my desk.

She walked off through burning dust
and fields, he said. Down through
hollows cut by quick spring floods,
floods that turned old graves to sunken
beds, forgotten, nursling, unmade beds.
She parted wires, eased her body through,
her breasts, her birthing hips, her one
good dress, up one fearsome hill, pine
and sun and shale, and down another.

A bible and an apple in her sack,
he said. A blanket, he supposed. Children
left to grow by juddering lantern light,
snow-light that crept like wolves
across the Plains, the seamless, hounded,
womanish Plains. And time went on. A day.
Two years. Another life. Wives went off
like that, he said—Sioux Falls, Billings.
Anywhere they'd never seen. Walking,
walking, to explain their muttered
flaring selves to no one.

FIRE IN THE NORTH COUNTRY

Every living thing speaks of fire,
even the fog smolders with ashes.
The sun: blood-lit. The sky crackles with it.

Now I see why I worshipped you, who lived without pity
or regret. You smoldered, rust-red in July.
I was small, held together by nothing.

I worshipped you like an answer. You who took
and bestowed like an addict. I was nothing,
barely held together. My charms: smoke and afflictions.

An addict, my mouth filled with thirst. If you were a woman
I'd admire you. If you were a horse I'd ride. O arsonist,
flame-thrower, burning down the scalded air:

See that we were children, wanting only to be fed,
the way a forest feeds on fire. As it is, I fear you:
though I keep you near, like a fever.

The place we live in has yellow walls and
light switches. We race along the halls,
a machine for washing, a machine for toast.
Others take their breakfasts, too,
in houses just like ours, a voice away.
Yes, please, with margarine, I say,
and wake each morning with hatred
in my throat, and snakes and stones
I'd like to hurl against my sister.

The linoleum in Mama's kitchen,
its russet squares, shone with wax
declaring Norwegian industry (or
maybe dread) and stood up to the claws
and shit of our proliferating kittens,
those little missile heads. When Mama
seared my goldfish in sudsy water—
I'd left it in a jar next to the sink—I cried
until she gave me a small blue velvet
box that once kept her wedding ring.
We held the funeral in the garden
among nasturtiums.

Later, it was my job (I believed it was)
to take our collie Kobuck to the vet
to put her down. She was old and
stumbled when she meant to run. I
stood behind the counter while they
took her through a door. She'd turned
to me, her dull brown eyes a naked
utterance. At home I put the fear
away, or meant to.

Where are they now, those furry
beings we chased around the house,
their litters born beneath our beds,
their crusted bowls, their dirty
cages? They let us seem the masters
of their sovereign village. They
licked our wounds. Swam in tactful
circles. Made life silkier, who
carried their wordless young
between their teeth. Showed us
the door where death is.
Named us human.

NOW THAT MORNINGS ARE COLD AGAIN

The neighbor's rooster doesn't know dawn
from a thousand stars, sleep all muddled
with vigilance. Easy to mistake the light
for an orchestra. Easy to get lost, unfurl,

call out at the wrong moment. When we
wake in the morning the air is wet,
and from black boughs a squirrel
hurls cones to ground, ardent earthquakes.

The way you feel when you fly cross-country,
entering a cloud, fields disappearing. Supermalls,
a river, nuclear reactors. Roads enthralling
girls to go. It's all down there, though

you're full of doubt, though you tremble.
On chilly mornings like this, I pull on a sweater,
sit at an altar. We know nothing, or who
when we turn, will come to us.

AVATAR

Last night, drifting near sleep's
shrouded coast, I returned to
my own first days, the wonder that
washed over me, my arrival from
the cloistered heat, wet, unknown,
headlong into the world, the startling
gulp of air, and how my mother
dressed me in a cotton gown,
swaddled me in flannel,
a nameless one, bound, unfledged,
and brought me home and in the slow
undertow of her chaptered sleep
carried me from room to room,
pastel light of snow in every glass,
ice disquieting the hours,
and laid me down, ran her small
thick country hands the quick
interval of me, hands grown used
to parting dark from dark, to
wash and powder me, the way
I went with her, alone, at night,
when I would cry, to rock and
suck and fall into the careless
beauty of that once-given sleep—
fathomless, those standstill hours—
when I was just a little one,
the cooing vowels that tied us
fast to what words later
could not say, while I grew
fat on milk, her world-round
breasts, her arms a second womb,
my aviator, my avatar, she ferried

me through whispered air, and how
she settled on a name, Ruth,
companion of the wanderers,
the sorrowing, and fixed me to
the Earth, those long winter
nights of my becoming.

THAT WILLOW

Above that willow only stars, and we lay
under, two whispered girls, half-blind
in the half-light, the long occult
branches, cool seep of earth against
our backs. Hatchlings, our breasts not
even breasts yet, bee stings, tender
as the mouth we saw Marilyn Monroe
make in the movies. Mandy Goodpasture,
Mandy Goodpasture, girl I chased
into a swayback barn to kiss on heaps
of fresh-shorn hay, and loll about
in sifted light. Those ravening hours:
O girl who kissed me back,
where are you now?

Under the willow we looked up
to see the stars fall one by one,
counted them, kept score, wanting
only to defeat each other. I imagined
in that great expanse my life
unwinding into space until I disappeared
and only stone and fire—voiceless,
mountain cold, full of real mercy—
remained. I could not account for it,
the way it held and cast me out,
as if it breathed me. That tree:
I saw it had been cut down when
I drove by, its groan, gone under
a neighbor's saw, the stars it carried
in its crown falling a second time. And
in the yellow grasses, the place where
we lay dreaming, the years we
traveled distantly already in us.

DO YOU CONSIDER YOURSELF A NATURE POET?

When I woke up, I drank a glass of water
that came from the clouds, the ocean,
the river that swept through the city
I'd slept in. I drank it down, cold,
into my body. I walked along streets
and under leaves and knew I loved
without effort the light that fell
on the branches crossing like
veins on the back of the earth.
The trees kept me walking on my
two legs, as they walked on theirs.

Tonight, I look up at stars scattering
salt through the indigo sky;
unbroken; through time. An old
habit of theirs, to lean down and
hover. The breeze that followed me
all day has given way, and I know,
once more, the terror of being.

ROAD TRIP

We roll south and east, past fields
of ripening hops and wheat, high
plateaus fashioned from forgotten seas.
Knuckled apple trees. A *for sale*
sign flapping at a mothballed
missile site. The river where we
knelt to kiss the mineral rush
of clear cold water.

In a campground a flock of children
dart beneath the pines. Their voices
echoing against basalt. Why is it
now that I remember them,
of all the ones we left behind?
The way their words chimed,
calling us to look. I want
to say they remind me
of breaking glass, the way they
traveled privately and bare skinned
into the belly of their lives, not
innocent—we never were—full
of harm and yearnings, pitiless,
proud, unhinged from time. Only
the seasons turned, only sun.
Only our bodies
dragging us deeper.

Love, death, heat, gasoline.
An apple ripening on a slender stem,
the makings of a garden where
no other than the Other lives,
the one you'd come to love if

you would love yourself,
the child sleeping
in the dark. Bees pilot in from
ruined hives, their silver throats
tin cups to drink the world's
suffering. Stench of slaughterhouse.
Pumpjacks in the fields, sexless
beasts against the sky.
It's a fragile art
to breathe and settle deep
into faux leather seats beside
your lover, a slender moon,
sober, crossing Lolo Pass,
eighty miles an hour,
just after midnight.

YELLOWSTONE

Even the rivers he'd stood in
remembered his shadow.
They carried it wherever they went,
flowing north and east,
hurrying over downed trees,
under ice. They took him along.

The day my father died
he said, Let me lie down,
put a blanket on me. Play me
a song. Yes, that one, he said.
Stars cast a sturdy net over
the place he was walking.
Lying down, hard breathing,
he was like a man climbing
an avalanche by moonlight.
Crusted, hard, breaking down.
Tough work, his going.

Watch for the others,
we whispered. Carry our
greetings to them if such
currents run there. Here is
your canteen. Your pens, a compass.
A small mirror to hold the world
you are walking away from.
Take these along in your
pockets. The others will
know what to do. They've
done it already.

But we didn't know,
ourselves, not anything
much. Only how hard he
worked right up to the end,
burning it all, everything
into the flames, throwing
on splits of cottonwood
and pine.

THE OLD COUNTRY

You went like this, without a map,
apart, seeing what was there.
The grass humming with glad
apian hunger, a single cloud
appearing and drifting away.
Over there, it said.

No one says, though sometimes
their eyes tell of it. A hand
circling blue cloth on china plates,
a skater on ice. How could they
help but sing of the geese in
the meadows and marshes each spring,
white feathers dipped in black
like a pen in its ink well.
Wings above the floating
snowfields of the mountains,
those years before even
the gods walked there.

URSA MAJOR PROWLS THE CHUGACH RANGE

I howled, they said, when I was
born, and woke the other babies
in their bassinets. Breath heaved me
to the antiseptic mess, the glare, my
mother's breast. I was daughter two.
The other one already clung to Mama.

O what Arctic dark raged down
to rake away the moon and fill my mouth
with snow. Caribou shook stars from sky,
I heard their hooves engrave the iron ice.
Spirit-licked, daubed red, I heard my
mother's cry. That howl. I joined her.

LETTER HOME

> The town has become accustomed to the war
> in the way one can get used to old age,
> the thought of death, to anything at all.
>
> —*Sándor Márai*

We said we'd be old like our uncles,
have girls who wouldn't leave us.
Now this instead. Another country
under my boots, sand the color of bones
ticking against my helmet. Some days I feel
I'm at the beginning of time,
the Imperial Star Destroyer hurling
away without me. I can't remember
the smell of my own room. Remind me
the color of Mom's eyes when you write.

Day after day rage enters me like a god
or machine, even in my dreams.
Without it I couldn't go on.
The terrible things we say we'll do,
we say without shame like a football
chant. When the guy next to me cried out
I thought of the train near home,
the way it feels to stand close
as it goes by. Like the sound of a horse
breathing—it came out of him—the air
so hot, the world tumbling backwards
like a bright Millennium Falcon. Strange
how quiet, and the sun in the sky
where it always was. The guy
moaned. I put my mouth over

his mouth the way they showed us. I
pressed my hand against the wound.
This place: different than what
they said. I followed him all
the way to stone.

CYCLING

We clipped a deck of playing cards
to silver spokes with clothespins pilfered
from her cotton bag. Our engineering
turned us proud. We were small,
wanting only to hear the
click-click-snap of flapping cards
as we picked up speed across the asphalt.

That's not quite true, I wanted to belong
to you, my brothers, as we set off into
the heat, the long disappearing hour
of rusting light at summer's end. We
were made of that, of sunburned
backs, of light and fear, and flawless
knees that pumped as fast as we
could go. And we went fast.

It was a spare and lonely road
our people took. House by house,
those separate lives, suburban in their
troubles, and alike. We were
small, wanting only the brilliance
of one day. I rode with arms flung
out to eat the air and feel the shush
of time against my body. And you,
nearly twins, rode side by side,
whistling. Vanished into purple dusk
and came back around as men.

TELLING TIME

for my father

Tonight I stood outside, named
the stars you'd named for me. Dug
out maps that'd told you how to go.
My actions, you once said,
let those stand for me.

This morning your old Timex
stopped. It had chirped
every afternoon at 4:15, to ready
you for supper. I'd worn it on my wrist
for months, its greeting like a shade
pulled up in winter to let
the last light of day pour in. It sent
a quick small word beneath a river.
Plum, it said. Or axle.

I held it to my ear, heard water
seep from a Cretaceous sea that
once covered all this rangeland.
Arrowheads, a buffalo horn
found on the ranch. You took
those with you. Now you've gone
further than you ever drove
on two-lane highways.

KLIPSAN BEACH

The dunes hollowed me out
and gave me back to the sun

and I set out for the edge
of the continent, that ceaseless

grinder of stone, the Pacific
with its cave-blue succulence,

tasting of Japan, wave
after wave, the tangled grasses

a child's hair after sleep.
And later, to sit on the deck

in the shadows of pines
and nap in maritime air—

it felt lavish, aimless—my friends
cooking dinner. It was enough.

And in that amplitude, I could
grieve again. I could long for you.

II The Country I Come From

THE COUNTRY I COME FROM

for Everett Hunt

A two-track road crosses over the prairie lands of the Great Sioux Reservation and the Article 16 Unceded Indian Territory, by right of the Fort Laramie Treaties of 1851 and 1868. The treaty lands in present times are called Wyoming, Montana, and the Dakotas. My Welsh-English grandparents (white people) homesteaded between the Powder and the Little Powder River, in Wyoming, in 1916, on a piece of treaty land (settlers: given land).

My cousins grew up in South Dakota, members of the Mnicoujou band of the Lakota (land taken). Here, my cousins continue to live—ranchers, a beautician, a bar owner, teachers, a quilter—on Cheyenne River Sioux Tribe lands. Land crossed by people who walked slowly across the badlands in winter—men, women, children; the old ones; the little ones—through a confluence of utterances and the exclamations of birds. Along stream beds and iced creeks. Making their way south to join Lakota relations at Wounded Knee, 1890.

The voices herein are made of scraps, rumors, whispers, imaginings. Stories.

I KATHRYN HUNT

These are the roads I take
when I think of my country.
The hills like a small girl,
heedless and dreamy.
A sea of grasses. Wind
coving the breaks. My father's
 ashes strewn here.

I hadn't thought of
the sweet bitter sage
seeping into the air
as they walked.

Where are the Indians?
I asked Grampa Vern.
I was six, maybe seven.
Ain't no Indins, he says.
I (white) know better.
I watch *Wagon Train*.

II

The whale, albatross, mastodon
woke from Nothing into This: An incandescence
of meteors trailing the scent of a wrecked
star-mother. The earth an inheritance of
sea-churn and wet peaches as round
as a vowel. A dream, a movie, all shadow
& light. Like a cottonwood leaf in spring,
life comes back green and it speaks.

III VERN HUNT

The poorhouse turned me out
of South Dakota and I rode west
to the Little Powder. The land
the government conferred, me and
Pearl proved up, and I put a herd
of whiteface on it. Didn't hurt me
none to ride all day, or sweat. I was
young. The land was mine. It's true
I once near beat to death a horse
that failed me in a ditch. Beat it
with a stick, my son hollering.
I turned my brother's
widow off his land
for what he owed me.

Life twists you like a rope.
I stood steady in the shambles:
No one could ever say I'm nobody.
That sonofabitch Roosevelt
brought power all the way to
Tennessee. But on the Little
Powder we burnt kerosene clear
through to nineteen-fifty-eight.

IV

The seed wheel turns and the air itself
tastes of snow & sleep. The grasses
lie down. The horns of the mountains
rise from the body of the plain, further
away than memory.

Winter is repose; given, gravid.
What else are hands for but to warm
one another with tenderness?

The wheel turns toward the sun
once a day. And then into the dark.
That the two-legged nose-breathers
may learn how to stand
within all they don't know.

V PEARL WATKINS HUNT

Vern? I knew he was trouble but I
went anyway when asked. Where
else could I belong? The first
born dead. The next one, I took the train
to Mother's. Spring, she sent us
back to him, my tiny boy a shiny thing.
My second son, a neighbor lady tended
me in our cabin, while the men played ball
out in the pasture. I heard *thwack-thwack*
from where I lay, the way they cheered,
while I beseeched it out of me.
After that I sought to keep him
off me.

A knot of sparrows panicked
up the sky when I went out at dusk
to call my boys in. Mornings, always
chores and I went on.

VI

If dangerous: then fog & obsidian.
If wounded: butterfly weed.
If thirst: the Yellowstone, the Powder,
    the Missouri, the Cheyenne.
If hunger: Duck Potato, hiŋhaŋ́ tahaŋ́pe.
If snake bit: úŋglakčapi.
If sex: the dark pools of the eyes.
If birth: a swarm of earthquakes.
If lonely: consider the flight of the vulture.
If beauty: a herd of pronghorn.

VII HATTIE BIRD WATKINS

When I saw those white marks
on the board I felt God had given
them to me alone. I turned all
twenty-six letters in my own small
hand by Christmas.

We ate salt on bread,
a little oil if Mama had it.
At seventeen, I went to Laramie
for normal school, then schooled
my own. I spent summers
with my sisters on the porch.

Vern claims he asked me first,
but he'd have taken any girl
who'd set her name on Indian
bones. Wyoming was strewn
still with arrowheads and
scraping stones. Six hundred
forty acres for Vern. Six hundred
forty for Pearl. She went with him.
I went on to California.

VIII

Stone-headed bison
as plentiful as stars
thunder-rocking the high
tundra of Alaska
clear down to the grasslands
of Mexico, across the birdsong
prairies of the Plains,
on to the Appalachians,
their colossal hearts
flooding over riverbeds & steppes,
jumping & dancing,
Pleistocene years.

IX WILLARD HUNT

Our lives out there
was a furnace of hours.
I seen plenty quarter-sawn
cabins fall to nothing
on the Powder, roofs
and men tore open to sky.
Never once knew what to
make of any of it. Sheep,
sundered fences. Our tongues
good as ashes. Our backs
all we had. Hardly enough
at the end to remember.
Seems like hate was all
that protected me.
Never had no help.

X

An antediluvian river tugging its banks,
the way a child tests the hand hold of his father.
Rainclouds fuel the muddy river,
gut-rock rumbling down the river's
long fluent back into crevasse,
aquifer, arroyo, sea.

Before breakfast a woman nods at Death,
stirs the oatmeal, feeds her kids.
Stands with them under
cold generous rain.

XI MERCY LOUISE HUNT

I never heard anyone ever speak of love.
What would that be but a fancy card
sold down at Milford's. Under all those
gravestones I wonder if you'd ever find
two who knew the blesséd sympathy
love is said to be.

Closest I ever came was
Marie Poplawski, a Polish girl.
Her name meant small loaf of bread.
We swam at night in the river,
our cotton dresses scraps
of clouds caught in the willows,
and dressed ourselves
without a single word—

XII

Meadowlark, owl. The valiant
red-tailed hawk. Wind-gathering
wings over swales & beer cans
& bale wire. For something will
always rise up and fall again.

Ancestors fly between,
carrying letters to scatter on
the other side of the pond.
A silver barn in a field.
Fall chill in the hunters.
Why do the snow geese
swoop & holler so?

XIII INA EAGLE SHIELD DUPREE HUNT

There's a swallowed-up place
between my ribs.
That's how I say it. Iyókogna.
In-between world.
I lived there all my life.
What part of me
did they wish me to forsake?
I was born of all of them,
the ones-who-killed,
the slaughtered ones.

I dwell by the river,
Mníšoše. Mnicoujou.
Frenchmen in the way back.
Each bit of me someone
always telling me was bad.
I knew the Indian words
but taught my little ones to
speak American. For Pahá Sápa,
say Black Hills. Ipákšaŋ,
a bend in the river.

I married Roy Hunt and he
made my allotment lands
take to cattle. My sons
learned it. He sat in bars
in Rapid, and I raised eleven
children on Dupree Creek.
I had a fast-running horse.
Šuŋglúzahaŋ.

XIV

The wreak and suck of time,
a storm pounding in from far away like pestilence.
The willful amnesia of the settler class.
Abolished songs, annulled lives and ways:
the flame & flume of history. A convocation of voices
unheard—agonies, stories, lies, rumors—
except for an urgency of wind
that gathers them in.

XV ROY HUNT

Sure I liked my whiskey neat.
I ate dust enough chasing steers
for the Leaf outfit. We was paid
three dollars dawn to dark. Drove
the herd down the Little Powder
all the way to Moorcroft to load
them up for slaughter. I had a
better thought. I went to
Eagle Butte and married
Ina Eagle Shield. Ina went to
Christian church but doctored us
the Indin way. Me and her had
nine pretty Indin girls and
two no-count Indin boys.

The land she got
for being Sioux,
one hundred sixty acres.
Dawes Act. We added on.

I'd have sold that land but
Ina made me sign it
to our youngest boy and him
a schoolteacher, see, thinking
he knew something. Schooling
Blackfeet in Montana, sweating
it out in one of them sweat
lodges. Like he was somebody.

XVI

Now is the whistling hour,
dark settling over the burnt fields
of despair. Souls & animals
whittle-way through teeth-clatter
& burrowed blood-sweat,
night's flowering harmonies.
Even the black Sun howls
with terror.

XVII SOLOMON EAGLE SHIELD DUPREE HUNT

They say I chased my dad around
the ranch and if that's true
the reason was my wanting him
to see me. He had spurs and leather
chaps. I wanted those. They all
wore them. My uncles.
They'd come around, though
Vern he always slept wrapped
in a soogan in his truck.
What did I know?
I was chasing round the ranch,
all smiles and mischief.
But stories get told in
lots of ways and I couldn't
hold on to those he left on me,
my dad, Roy Hunt. Not if I wanted
to survive. *No good Indian* is what
he'd say and spit it out like I
was a thing you wouldn't want to
touch. I was his son and I
still don't know why a man
would leave his mark
on his own boy like that.

XVIII

The Arctic wind has
an Inuit name. The prairie's
vocation—to lie beneath
the bitter cold. Far into
the mystery, farther
than thought.

Two lovers in a pickup
whispering
their oldest stories,
a wool blanket and
a sorta-works heater.
That fire.

Who can explain it,
the joy a constancy of light
can bring to the heart?

XIX ROSE MCCOWAN HUNT

My folk's land gave out,
we never had no other piece
our own. I learned to hunt,
trap. Sold furs just to get by.
Once, Happy left me with
a thousand sheep on open
range down near Gillette. He
went visiting that Fitzpatrick
girl in Garryowen. Late at night
coyotes whittled down the edges
of the herd, I'll not forget
their screams.

Another time I trapped
an old coyote, chased him
down a hill, my trap hanging
from his front leg. He ran
upright like a man. He hid in
willow by a creek. That's
where I caught the flash
of his eyes, his *yes*. I finished
him with a rock.

XX

Their hearts—Fractured by the kick of a horse.
Their hearts—Rough hackle.
Their hearts—A river lit with ice.
Their hearts—A woman looking for her child in snow.
Their hearts—Struck by the unreasonableness of Love.

XXI ALBINA HUNT

I stayed behind in Mama's house.
Ice crawled up the window panes.
The potatoes in the bin went
soft past saving. I knew there was
another world. I'd seen two sisters
and three brothers cross that
muddy river and not return. I
envied them, the way they
turned their backs on us.
Mama grew thin as smoke.
Papa as he always ever was—
silent as a man. From our
opal windows I watched
year chase year around.

XXII

In the slaughterhouse of history,
a thousand yellow leaves
twist in afternoon sun.

The technologies of weapons
and the metabolism of greed.
Curses laid upon the iron earth.

The merciless balefire
of the Hotchkiss gun, where they were
gathered at Wounded Knee.

Who dreams the dreams
of the ones whose bodies
the bullets found?

XXIII LILLIE EAGLE SHIELD DUPREE

I've grown light as a thread.
Stitch by stitch I went along each quilt.
I sewed dresses for the pow wow dancers.
Elk teeth. Beads and jingles from China. One stitch,
two stitch: I'm a scrap the wind is busy carrying off.

The Indian name that Mother gave, I remember.
I keep it here. Up there, behind them dark
thunder clouds. Now days the little Head Start
kids learn to speak Indian. Lakota. Taŋyáŋ yahí.
Welcome. I spread broken pieces on
my table to make quilts for all the babies.
Their wants wash over me in sleep.
I hear the storm rifling the prairie,
the river inside the river.

XXIV

For whom the grass is a bed,
who carried the passed-along words in their mouths,

walked upright in their bones
across the under-foot tomb of earth.

Milky Way in the two-track sky—
dark embracing the dark.

Flesh of the wild current
sealed with grief,

time onto time,
lit sentience within.

XXV KATHRYN HUNT

On the prairie time
burns straight through,
no mountains to stop it.
Leaves eavesdrop on
the words of the wašíču
treaty signatories. Out of the
corner of my eye I see them.
They move with the sound
of shod horses.

And there, in an abeyance
of days, under the roots
of fallow grasses,
three hundred songs,
one for each season of silence.

And in the blue stubble
of winter, behind a listing
fence and a field of gates opening
into memory, the bones
of the wind-blessed dead,
the color of sand. They
weigh nothing at all.

III Migrations

MIGRATIONS

The pale-yellow blossoms
of the hellebores remind us
of winter's long resolve.

In the south, the Western Tanager
is aflame with nectar. Wasps,
cicadas, love. Bird camouflaged as
guitar lick, a zodiacal sunrise.
Smoke from smoldering tires
in the valley of Oaxaca.

Come, ungovernable blaze.
Little god. Summon us.
Torch the naked branches.

We stamp our feet, say good year
to those we see in woods beside
the silver-plated pond, each one of us
made almost holy by our longing.

By afternoon the passing light
is smoke, and shadows
caves in which we hardly breathe.
Chill-stung leaves shrill as
cellophane. Ground—boot hard.

Under a bright affinity of stars
I wake to hear an owl calling
from the branches of a fir, its cry
reaching through the silence that
enfolds us. The dead eavesdrop
from their distant drafty offices, still
curious, still brave, with the humility
of lichen. Each one alight with love
they cannot help but bear.

SPRING EQUINOX

You must take up your oar and go on a journey . . . .

—*Tiresias to Odysseus*

A thousand thousand wings rise and turn
in borrowed light. Brants, swans, pintails.
Scurrying dunlins on the shore. Huckleberry
in woodland shade, where hummingbirds
obey the frantic swell of spring, the lush
unfolding rush of the Great Turning.

Yet I despair to see
spring come around, unstoppable as rain.
Runnels with their muddy flood,
daffodils in every garden. The season
will not stop for me, for what I'd will
to do, or haven't done, and all those
years spun into other years, and gone.

"Our friend," "Our father," on gravestone,
men drowned in Shoalwater Bay,
1878, out in a storm come sudden up
to take them. I wander on the shore,
startled by the slanting sun. My wanting
heart that fed on dreams, refuses now
the promises of spring. I take up my oar.

DR. KILDARE

My sister and I sat on Mama's white Naugahyde couch
after school. Our legs stretched out, our bare feet in the middle,
not touching. Watching TV.

We were schooled in not saying.

A soap opera, Dr. Kildare. That kind, fine-looking man
in his white jacket.

We loved him with the smoldering passion
of the female young. That is to say, with love that could not be
requited. That agreed to remain invisible.
Not needing anything.

His hands reached out. The way he spoke to the nurses and patients,
sympathetic, though strangely apart.
No matter their anguish.

We had cause to be alarmed by the conduct of men.
Men had shown us the dangers.

The man who came to the door
with a pistol, looking for his wife. Mama backed him down
with icy nonchalance. Or was it her formidable charm?

The boyfriend who put a gun
to my sister's head and spun the chamber.
Let's see if it's loaded, he said.

The looks, the hands, the punishing insistence.
Common flavors.
Their steely remove, like the door of a commercial freezer.
Their silence like newspapers
that had never been printed.

How small we felt submerged in their laughter.
How we loved and hated and pitied them.

Years later we learned Dr. Kildare was gay.
We'd felt safe with the doctor, a man we didn't need
to worry about.
Dr. Kildare was vulnerable, hidden.
A rabbit, an animal like ourselves.

We knew only how to hide what frightened us
somewhere no one could see.
Where no one could smell the blood.

How does a woman learn to stand
and reflect on her own life, the way a doctor
stands in a sickly-green hallway considering a difficult case?

We were unschooled.
What any wounded animal was given to do, we crawled into the underbrush.
Like beautiful Dr. Kildare.

We hid from each other though we slept side by side.
Anyone came near us,
we hid from them.

READING HAMLET

Utterly empty, utterly a source . . .

—*Seamus Heaney*

When the others were asleep, sometimes
in the silence she took *Hamlet* from the shelf
and read aloud the scenes where he
renounced poor staggering Ophelia,
or stalked the predawn hours, consumed,
wild to know who spilt his father's blood.
And I would yawn and drift and nod
until she sent me off to bed. "One kiss,"
she'd say and I'd begrudge her, who'd shown
my father out the door, the dark play of
that between us. In the moon-mown hours
of her dying, only the poems she'd given me,
the boundless anguish of a prince. Never
nearer than those far-off castled nights.

THE SUMMER YOU IMAGINED ME

Nine months I listened to that
love-dove song that tumbled us along.
Light heaped up against the birch
and ash, your favorite hour. I breathed
you in through gills, lived in shallows
beneath your ribs. Salt in those first
open channels between us. Bracken,
and wild ginger. I was a mineral
gleam stirring.

Mama, I know your stories
better than I know my own. The
riverbank where you foraged blackberries
with a friend. The hurrying current
that carried off your dead. Even
to ourselves we are changelings
made of wind. Those old griefs:
Let's ask a mountain to walk
with them awhile. *Once we sat beneath
a wall,* you wrote. *Contented. Seen.*
The summer you imagined me.

WATER CHILDREN

That awful *thunk* and suddenly the arrival
of the minus hour, the quick undoing of
small beings. Feathers, beak, bone,
it's one quick eye eyeing me.

An intemperate sweep of narcissi and ferns—
all this glory notwithstanding. The way words
put down on paper disappear to nothing,
glyphs in mud. I left it there to die.

How like birds the waiting ones who
hover near, the ones I brush against at night.
They visit from a world away, accompany me,
who might have been a mother. The way

words appear from nowhere, falling through
branches to scent, disturb, quicken life. Later
I returned to find the sparrow gone, roused
back to sky. Or taken by a cat. A hand-sized

throb I'd found between the falling and
the rising world, at the holy-moly opening
of day. Near and slight, that crack; ajar.

LAST CHANGES

His hands were still
as lake water. An old song
told us what to do. I'd seen
his hands slide through green
water once, lift three-pound
trout, spoon-bright, moon-
mouths agape. And after the fish
had been thrown back—their
glazed beauty, that sudden lost
camaraderie. And I stood,
dry-eyed, dumb, burning
in the hush and watched
his hands, his endless
going from the boat.

She took from the closet her old
two-piece suits, the ones she
bought before we came along,
just after the war. She was wearing
a half-slip and a merry widow,
and placed her shoes on the floor
near my feet. Big clunky carnal heels.
Padded shoulders on the jackets.
Pencil skirts with high happy slits—
smooth gabardine wool. Even I,
a panicky ten-year-old girl, could tell
my mother's suits were persuasive.

One by one she stepped into them,
turned to show me, so I could see
the careless post-war glamour
of the hems, their matrimonial elegance.
Styles, she said, as if imparting the secret
of secrets to her larval, disloyal daughter,
come back around. Someday, these will
all be back in fashion. Her hazel eyes
shone with uncommon glee.

Then she hung her suits back in the closet
and slipped into her robe, the one
with cigarette burns down the front
like a broken necklace. Laid a cotton
shirtwaist dress over a chair beside
her four-inch heels. In the morning
she would shepherd the four of us off
to school, then head to her job,
a secretary at the Boeing Company.

On the kitchen counter she'd leave
four paper sacks, lined up,
a peanut butter sandwich, an apple,
sometimes a note tucked inside.
I love you, it'd say. I'd find it
at school and feel ashamed.
I didn't understand why.

Here, the sky is always changing.
The sun burning moisture off the leaves.
The rain evaporating, perfuming
the whole day, washing away something
I don't even have a name for. A word
that will tell how it is.

About those suits and the cyclical nature
of women's fashion—I thought
my mother was wrong,
that I knew better.

Last night I stood on the porch
while shadows flooded around my ankles,
the wind in the trees like a river.
What collects in silence was there too.
I knew she had tried to tell me
what I'd need to know. Her words open
inside me still, coming and going in cycles
like women's fashion. So I'd be ready,
she said. Wool gabardine one year,
wash 'n wear polyester the next.

MY FIRST GARDEN

My mother was dying
and I made a garden
outside my door.

Only her dying and
a garden. Only dying
and sowing. My mother

was dying and I put
seeds in the ground
to save myself.

By August, I had salvia,
sage, tender verbena.
Tall purple flowers.

Bouquet in hand I walked
behind. Not near medicine
enough. But I took it.

DEMETER IN HER REALM

I am a slaughterer of yellow chickens, I take their small
stinking lives in my hands.

I am the one bone-tired of being bone-tired.

The one who does not know the way out.

I am the one in four-inch heels walking between desks
and Xerox machines, avoiding their hands.

Today already I changed five catheters
and cleaned up the shit of an old woman.

Bruises. Here, between my legs.

Nine children, mine, from this body.

I feed others with these hands. If they say thanks,
OK. If they don't, OK too.

A rock on top of me.

I count out dollars and dimes all day. Only
a few given me.

I have not heard my daughter's voice in seven years.
Her sweet angry voice.

I am the one who walked away from you because I could.

I do not speak your language.

WHAT RITUALS DID YOU PERFORM?

When you were gone, I draped black bunting
over doors, rent my clothes, walked bare
breasted down the empty asphalt streets.
Cut off all my hair, turned back the clocks
to set their silly faces running toward

the time before. Ripped out
the telephone. Wore a veil to show
the world, turned the mirrors
to face the wall. And kept a thousand
candles burning.

You'd shown me how, you'd done it
for your own dead. Your mother gone
while you were in the cradle. Your brother
lost at sea. Your father and that lonesome
business with the gun.

When you were gone, I prayed. I called
down blessings on your life. I held a wake,
invited everyone, served poppy cake.
I played your favorite songs. And still
I woke and found you gone.

DRIFT, BOAT

1

You sleepwalk from our bed
to picture window, the neighbors'
roofs turned sandbars in an
ebbing sea: You've been gone
to Bristol Bay another season,
and the flare of headlights climbing
up the hill seem to you to trace
the flashing backs of silver sockeye.
Fish tangle to their gills, your arms
haul fifty-fathom nets. Salmon
gather toward the Egegik, that
final dash to spawning ground,
fresh water in their blood.

2

Lie down next to me. We're older
now, and when we feast it is
to take into our bodies the oblivion
of wild northern amplitude again.
Your hands, your mouth, our salted
skin. I want to feel the ancient
current take us. Not the childhood
country of savaged forests, clotted
streams. But the bedrock, bliss-
dark soundings of the body.

WHERE ARE YOUR GLOVES, ANNA?

> But I warn you:
> this is my last existence.
>
> —*Akhmatova*

All day Maryna and I walked
the streets of St. Petersburg.
The oily waters of the Neva bore
your face, terror, clouds. We heard
the pleadings of the doomed at
Kresty Prison, saw women pass
packages for the dead to the jailers.
The stone walls of the prison
made us children again.

Mayakovsky pointed the way
to your apartment cluttered
with pots, a small bed, bereaved
light. Your lovers and son
stood watch in the garden.
Nadezhda cluck-clucked
like a hen, her mind inscribed
with songs of the vanished.

Oligarchs on six continents
shiver when the iron bell of
your voice reaches them, Anna.
The same booted men stride
the earth, East and West,
hunting for gold and for oil.
Your poems are seeds in the teeth
of the wind. Your gloves are
on the table with the newspapers
and jam, where you left them.

GRAVEL ROAD

A broken-necked warbler
on cool soil, its eyes

almost seeing, given over.
A house lifting and settling

in the wind. The place where the
women of my family gather bones,

the peak-roofed ossuary
a little house. The beds where

the old people wait. I hear
the long train of the hours

they spent in their pastures
or bending over a hot wood stove.

Pushing a hand truck down
a hospital corridor. With them

I enter the left-behind villages.
The lost babies. The drowned

fishing boats. The night they
looked out a window, wondering,

amazed. The day they held out
their hands to the telegram.

On my jeans sweet bone-ash
the wind has flung

back at me, that I might know
where I come from. That I

might know where
I'm going. That too.

WHAT COLOR IS THE STONE
YOU CARRY IN YOUR POCKET?

for Bryher: Basin, Montana

Afternoon slides away into the aspens by the creek.
Shadows plum the Elkhorn hills. Confusion,
or heartbreak—help them out of their brown
canvas coats. Offer them a chair.

At dusk five antelope muster near the willows.
Their obsidian horns candle the cooling air,
the damp grasses collecting all they need
for the night, heat giving way.

On the gravel road to High Ore, forsaken
cabins where night floods between the timbers.
Ferocious melodies ring out, and weeping, still,
as soft as a quartz pebble.

GRACE

Those stories of
childhood, once as
cruel and necessary
as a wall, tonight feel like
old coats emptied
of the body.

WHERE DO WE COME FROM?

for Luis Alberto Urrea

We can't say what a river is,
only that it throbs in our bones

and will never slake our longing.
Through a mountain pass,

down the long game trail,
across the salt plains.

Where an old sea spilled way, falling
into time. That place made itself,

the saguaro, the crazy flicker,
the two-legged nose breathers.

That maternal slit. The first
erotic going forth, everything

we'd need already in us. A shy
place that scorns our certainty.

Will not be seen or named.

ASH-BOAT

1

Each Wednesday noon the town
alerts us to disaster with five notes
from Close Encounters. They gentle us
toward our losses. What happens
in Japan reaches here, only higher.
Sun on waves, chill in November
ground. Each thing folded into
its other self.

Kathy's head is crowned in circling
elegance, paisley cloth woven in
Morocco lending her a way to marry
corresponding bewilderment of ease
and chemo into the telling of her day.
The waffles warm us through. We let
our talk raise a world whole enough
to touch. Any hour is fine
for maple syrup. Her husband stares
into a blue scattering of gulls, to forgive
himself toward a house he cannot
measure. The roof is off that place.

2

The park had been left to the animals,
and we walked in through a locked
gate as if into a chamber.
There was a lockdown on
and four of us walked in through
the brume, a convocation of eagles
in attendance, wing-wide, curious,

no one else on the beach.
Her husband arrived on a bike,
and together we walked toward
whatever was now locked away.
One carried a small boat he'd
fashioned for the occasion. Two
carried flowers. One carried a song.
One carried her ashes. We circled up
on the beach, the tide ebbing, the better
to carry her out, the rook circling
our ankles, and we had a song,
a poem, a prayer, some ashes.
All she would need. Offered them.
Were strangely elated. Ran along
the shore chasing the ash-boat
as the tide took it out and out and
pulled her bier past the surf, past
the islands of the Salish Sea. A boat
with her ashes, a white sail that
showed itself on the dark interior
of the sea now and again.

In Memorium, Kathy Francis

The hands went along with the body
wherever it went. They wept
when the body wept, trembled
each time the body fell silent
with pleasure or regret. Salt
left a trail on them. Babies
were entrusted to them, since
the hands were precise. And
enigmatic. Were they light beacons,
really? The hands opened calmly
like seeds, endured the passage
of time like a canyon.
Bejeweled, tattooed, they were
never hungry, not for melons
or experience or for the Ever
After. A seamless universe
had been given to their keeping.
In the orbit of their miraculous
digits: lust, lacerations, charms,
prophesies. And in their long
memory, from the bed of the blue
rivers that ran through them, the
hands drank their full measure,
and were empty, exalted.

NOTES

Page 10: For Steve Minkler, *In Memoriam.*

Page 25: For my brothers Bruce Hunt and Brian Hunt.

Page 27: For Marilyn Picariello and Linda Rose.

Page 29: The title is a line from Bob Dylan's *With God on Our Side.* My hands-down favorite rendition is by the Neville Brothers, on YouTube.

Page 29: "The Country I Come From" is for all my South Dakota, Wyoming, Montana, and Idaho cousins—through the generations.

GRATITUDE

This book would not have been possible without the support of a community of friends and fellow travelers. Thank you to Geo, my love and best friend—for the life we've made and the shelter you offer. My appreciation to the editors of magazines, journals, and anthologies who first published many of these poems. Eternal gratitude to Christine Holbert, publisher of Lost Horse Press, who scooped *Seed Wheel* out of the pile and designed a beautiful book around it. Willapa Bay AIR where I began these poems, Ucross where I finished. The Poetry Goddesses: Gayle Kaune, Sharon Carter, and Pam Dionne. Peter Pereira, Kathleen Flenniken, and the Seattle crew. Charlotte Pence for your kind and instructive read. Dear darling Spencer Reece for your friendship and insight. Andrea Carlisle and Meg Glaser for reading "The Country I Come From" early on, and your timely encouragement. Tree Swenson for reciting Hopkins's "Spring and Fall" while we walked in the woods. Tess Gallagher, Gary Lilley, and Alice Derry for your inspiration and companionship here on the Olympic Peninsula. Susan, Hilde, Adrienne, Sally, Cindy, Sonia, Lauren: on the wide-open road together. And finally, I'm indebted to Iris Eagle Chasing for her deep knowledge of Lakota and her long experience as a teacher and speaker of the language. I'm grateful for her suggestions and for making me laugh.